BONDAGE BROKEN

(Freedom From Compulsive Habits)

Craig Hill

Family Foundations International
P.O. Box 320
Littleton, Colorado 80160

Printed in the United States of America

All scripture quotations, not otherwise noted, appear in The New
American Standard Bible. The following versions have also been used:
The New American Standard Bible, The Lockman Foundation, 1960, 1962,
1963, 1968, 1971, 1973, 1975; *King James Version*, Thomas Nelson, Inc.,
Publishers; *The Amplified Bible*, Zondervan Bible Publishers, 1965, 12th
Printing, 1975.

First Printing 1989
Second Printing 1994
Third Printing 1998

CONTENTS

Chapter 1　　　　　　　　　　　　　　　　　**1**
　　Broken Bondage!

Chapter 2　　　　　　　　　　　　　　　　　**23**
　　Why have I been unable to
　　overcome my bad habits?

Chapter 3　　　　　　　　　　　　　　　　　**41**
　　What are the keys to break
　　the bondage?

CHAPTER 1

BROKEN BONDAGE

Have you ever wondered why it is that you **do** things that you don't want to do and end up **not** doing what you want? For example, many of us want to establish in our lives an early morning daily time to read the Word of God and pray. Commonly we have repeatedly purposed to establish a habit of doing so. The morning of the first day comes, and the spirit says, "Time to get up", but the flesh says, "Time to stay in bed and sleep." Then a battle ensues between our flesh and our spirit. Sometimes the spirit wins that battle, but often the flesh prevails. In fact, we often find that the things we want deep within we are not able to do.

We end up doing instead, things we **don't** want to do. Many of us are continually in bondage to habits and attitudes that we have tried to overcome: hatred, constant or very frequent anger toward others, lust, promiscuous sexual relationships, masturbation, drinking, addiction to drugs, smoking cigarettes. Maybe it is compulsive eating, dieting, exercising, shopping, spending, or maybe not telling the entire truth, criticizing, gossiping, or speaking unkind words to people. Even simple things like fingernail biting or excessive talking can be unpleasant compulsions. When any of these things become habits, they overcome us, and we find ourselves in bondage to them.

1

Paul describes this situation of life exactly in Romans 7:14-16:

> *"For we know that the law is spiritual; but I am of the flesh, sold into bondage to sin. For that which I am doing, I do not understand; for I am not practicing what I would like to do, but I am doing the very thing I hate. But if I do the very thing I do not wish to do, I agree with the Law, confessing that it is good."*

Paul says that he finds himself doing the very thing that he does not want to do. Basically, he is describing the bondage of a habit.

Many of us have tried to break the power of habits in our lives but have not been very successful at doing so. We thought that we could just volitionally **will** these things to go away, but they don't instantly disappear by willing them to go away. Have you ever tried to will hatred out of your heart? It is like willing yourself to go to sleep; the more you try to go to sleep, the harder it is. Many of these habits follow the same pattern. The harder you try to break their power, the more powerful they seem to become in your life.

How do these bondages occur? How do these habits become so entrenched in our lives that we seem to be unable to break their power? Through a series of probing questions, we will begin to see how these habits take hold in our lives and how we can appropriate God's power to free ourselves from them.

WHY DO I DO WHAT I DON'T WANT TO DO?

A woman once came to me and confessed that she had cheated on a test that I had given in a Bible school class. She had the answers to one of the questions on the test written down on a piece of paper in her Bible. The class had been allowed to use their Bibles during the test. Though the woman knew it would be wrong to use a "cheat sheet" which had answers on it, when she came to a question to which she did not know the answer, she was overcome by temptation and used the "cheat sheet". Later the Spirit of God convicted her of cheating. She repented, confessing it to me. She hadn't wanted to cheat, but she felt compelled and found herself doing the very thing that she didn't want to do.

Most of us indulge in bad habits not because we **desire** to do them, but because of a compulsion to do so. Not many wake up in the morning saying, "I think I'll do what I don't want to do today. I think I'll sin," or " I think I'll yield to this particular habit in my life today." No, we don't **desire** to sin; rather, we are compelled by something deep within us. Then, unable to fight the compulsion, we succumb to the habit.

If we find ourselves speaking forth something that is not true, usually it is not because we have done so by design. It is because something within us has compelled us, and we find ourselves doing the very thing that we don't want to do.

So there is an unconscious compulsion that motivates us to do the things that we don't want to

do. But, even more, this force compels us not to do the things that we are prompted to do by the Spirit of God.

WHAT DRIVES THE COMPULSION?

A key to the answer is found in Hebrews 4:1- 2:

> *"Therefore, let us fear, lest while a promise remains of entering His rest, any one of you should seem to have come short of it. For indeed we have had good news preached to us, just as they also; but the word they heard did not profit them,* ***because it was not united by faith in those who heard."***

Hebrews 4:9- 10 says,

> *"There remains, therefore, a Sabbath rest for the people of God. For* ***the one who has entered His rest has himself also rested from his works,*** *as God did from His."*

As I meditated upon these scriptures, the Lord began to show me that compulsions within us stem from a lack of peace in our souls. God has told us through these scriptures that there is a rest that He has for us. He desires for us to enter His rest. As a matter of fact, that's one of the promises of His covenant for the people of God.

Verse 10 says that he who has entered into God's rest has himself ceased and rested from his own works. But often we don't cease from our own works. We continue to do our own works, not finding the peace in our souls that comes only by resting in God. **When there is a lack of peace and a lack of rest in your soul, your flesh is compelled to do something to attempt to bring peace and comfort to your soul.**

In other words, if your soul is not resting in God, if your emotions are stirred up and not at peace, if your mind is not at peace and not resting in the Lord, then your flesh will be compelled to try to do something to bring peace to your soul. However, the things that your **flesh** tells you will bring peace never do bring you peace.

Your flesh is a hard taskmaster, making ever increasing demands in exchange for ever diminishing returns of peace. Your flesh says, "Just take a drink, and you'll have peace" or "Just take some food from the refrigerator, and it will bring you peace" or "Just smoke a cigarette, and it will bring you peace." Your flesh may say, "If you can just fulfill yourself sexually, it will bring you peace." But all these things are lies. They bring a measure of peace for a short time, but they don't bring any lasting peace. As a matter of fact, when you fulfill these things, they simply demand more from you, and peace is not brought into your soul.

Yet we mistakenly believe that if we fulfill the desires of our flesh, doing all that it demands, our emotions will come into peace. The truth is, only Jesus Christ can bring peace to our souls. By dwelling in Jesus Christ, we can enter into the rest of God.

WHY AM I NOT AT PEACE?

Let's look at the content of Hebrews 4:2, which describes the children of Israel. They did not enter the Promised Land, because they believed ten errant spies who told them that the giants were too strong for them and that they would be defeated if they went into the land. The multitude refused, of course, to believe Joshua and Caleb who saw the same things as the other spies, but came to the very opposite conclusion.

Now the Lord told the Israelites that He would give them the battle, but they were unwilling to believe what God said. Hebrews 4:2 says,

> *"For indeed, we have had good news preached to us, just as they also; but the word they heard did not profit them, because **it was not united by faith in those who heard.**"*

They heard the Word of God, but they didn't put faith in what God said. They put more faith in what the ten spies said. Hebrews 3:19 says,

*"And so we see that they were not able to enter **because of unbelief.** "*

As a result, they did not enter into God's rest, either.

The reason that we don't enter God's rest and the peace He has for us is because of unbelief in our hearts. It is because we don't believe that He is really faithful to bring us peace, to bring us joy, to meet our needs. We don't trust that He is our Source, that He really can give us the peace and joy and comfort in our souls that we desire. Instead, we obey our flesh and believe in its deceitful and empty promises of peace.

WHY AM I IN UNBELIEF?

Most of us haven't consciously chosen to be in unbelief. We want to believe God, but sin is deceitful. Hebrews 3:12, 13 says,

> *"Take care, brethren, lest there should be in any one of you an evil, unbelieving heart, in falling away from the living God. But encourage one another day after day, as long as it is still called 'Today,' **lest any one of you be hardened by the deceitfulness of sin.** "*

The deceitfulness of sin is a very tricky thing. When you are deceived, you don't realize that you are deceived. If you knew that you were deceived, you would no longer be deceived. You would have the knowledge of that deceit and could do something about it.

Hebrews 3:13 in the Amplified Bible says,

> *"But instead warn, (admonish, urge and encourage) one another every day as long as it is called Today, that none of you may be hardened [into subtle rebellion] by the deceitfulness of sin --[that is] by the fraudulence, the strategem, the trickery which the delusive glamour of his sin may play on him."*

So sin defrauds you with a strategy and a trickery to take you captive to itself. Sin in your flesh will rise up, promising you, your mind, and emotions all kinds of peace and satisfaction. But sin never delivers what it promises.

The Lord showed me four specific lies through which sin in our flesh is able to deceive our minds and our emotions:

(1) **You believe God is not faithful to you.** In order to be willing to believe what your flesh tells you, you first must believe that God is not faithful. You have to believe that He is not going to bring you comfort and peace. His Word says that He is faithful, that He is your Source, your Comfort, and your Peace. But you first believe a lie that says God is not faithful to you.

(2) **You believe the lie that the habit into which your flesh wants to draw you in bondage will satisfy something deep in your soul.** The sin in your flesh defrauds you by promising the peace and comfort that it doesn't deliver.

(3) **You believe that this habit is stronger than the power of Jesus Christ within you to break it.** You may have tried to break the habit many times. You may have prayed, begged, fasted, done many things, yet have remained bound by the habit. Then, as a result, you come to believe that the habit is actually more powerful than Jesus Christ in you.

(4) **You believe that the habit or wrong attitude is part of you, that it is just the way you are.** For example, if you have a habit of criticizing, you say to yourself, "I'm just a critical person. I've always been that way." You believe that the attitude or habit is your temperament or nature, that it's just who you are. You identify yourself with that habit as just being a part of you.

You probably haven't consciously decided to believe lies that enable a bad habit to be established. Rather, as you believe these four lies, a subtle deception takes root, and your heart becomes hardened. You believe that God isn't going to be able to bring you peace, because your experience in the past has been that He hasn't. You believe that the habit is going to bring you peace and comfort. You believe that the habit is more powerful than the power of Jesus Christ in you to break it. You believe that the habit is just you, a part of you, and is very deeply rooted within you. The ultimate lie is when you believe that it is, in fact, you, and, therefore, there is no way you can become free of it.

WHAT FACILITATES THIS DECEPTION?

Let's back up once again in the story to Hebrews 2:14,15. These verses give us the answer:

> *"Since then the children share in flesh and blood, He Himself likewise also partook of the same, that through death he might render, powerless him who had the power of death, that is , the devil; and might deliver those who through fear of death were subject to slavery all their lives."*

These verses explain that the devil has deceived people through the fear of death. Although Jesus made Satan powerless and took away from him the **power** of death, he still continues to control people through the **fear** of death.

Because we are tri-part beings, we fear three types of death - physical death, spiritual death (that one's spirit is going to die and be eternally separated from God), and soulical death (that one's emotions or intellect will die).

The fear of physical death controls many people. Most Christians don't fear physical death, because

Jesus Christ rose from the dead so that when we die physically, our spirits and souls go on to live eternally with Him.

Spiritual death is something that we don't need to fear, either, because Jesus Christ stripped the devil of his power to kill His Spirit. Our spirits are eternally alive through Jesus Christ through the incorruptible, imperishable seed that has been implanted in our spirits (1 Peter 1:23).

But one of the most subtle but powerful and motivating factors within us is the fear of death in our souls - that we might die in some area of our intellects, emotions, or wills. This is the fear that compels us to do the things that we don't want to do and prevents us from being able to do the things that we do want to do.

For example, if I come home late, I may be afraid that my wife will be angry at me. Essentially, I'm afraid that my emotional well-being is going to be destroyed. As a result of this fear, I might be compelled by my flesh to make up a lie that will keep her from being angry.

When a person is in bondage to a habit of drinking alcohol, his or her flesh is saying, "You will not be happy (will not have soulical life) unless you drink alcohol." The person believes the lie that the alcohol will bring him or her life and peace. The fear of the absence of life in the soul compels a person to do something that will bring life to his or her soul.

Matthew 16:24 says,

"Then Jesus said to His disciples, "If anyone wishes to come after me, let him deny himself, and take up his cross, and follow Me. For whoever wishes to save his life shall lose it; but whoever loses his life for My sake shall find it. For what will a man be profited, if he gains the whole world, and forfeits his soul? Or what will a man give in exchange for his soul."

In our English Bibles, verse 25 uses the word **life**:

"For whoever wishes to save his life shall lose it."

But in the Greek language, the original language of the New Testament, this word **life** is actually the word **psuche**, which is the same word used in verse 26 for **soul**. So Jesus is not talking about losing eternal life; He is talking about losing "soul life." Jesus says that whenever you seek to try to save the life in your soul, you lose the very life you are seeking to save. But whenever you lose your life for His sake, whenever you give up your own soul life for Him, you find the life of Jesus Christ. It comes forth from your spirit and floods your soul.

You won't find life in your soul unless you yield that life to Jesus. Then the **true** life of Jesus Christ in your spirit (not deceptions from your flesh about what gives you life) can come forth and flood your soul.

For example, an alcoholic woman is enslaved to alcohol due to the fear of death in her soul. She longs after peace and comfort and joy in her soul, but her flesh tells her constantly that only alcohol will bring that to her. That's not the truth. Jesus Christ wants to soothe the longings in her soul. Furthermore, He is the only One Who has the power to do so.

If the woman considers dying to her flesh and trusting God to bring her the peace and the comfort that she has been receiving through the alcohol, a terrible fear immediately rises up within her. She fears she'll perish or that she'll be so agitated or so nervous that she won't be able to stand it if she doesn't drink. The discomfort is so powerful that she is convinced that the only way to eliminate the discomfort is to drink.

These are lies from the pits of hell that are fed to her by her own flesh. It's poisonous deception that undermines her ability to trust God. It causes her to put her faith and trust in alcohol to bring her peace, rather than in the Lord Jesus Christ. Thus, she finds herself in the situation that Paul describes in Romans 7: doing the very thing that she hates, the very thing that she doesn't want to do. This is because she is a slave to the fear that she will perish if she doesn't do what her flesh tells her will bring comfort, peace, and joy.

And yet, her flesh constantly demands more in order to deliver the same comfort! She doesn't get free, but gets deeper into bondage, and never receives the very comfort, peace, and joy for which she so desperately longs. As Jesus explains in Matthew 16:25, she ends up losing the very life in her soul for which she strives.

WHAT ARE OUR DEEPEST FEARS?

Every one of us constantly asks two questions in life. The <u>first question</u> is, *"Am I of value in this world?"* We believe a lie that the devil feeds us: we are not valuable or important. Fear rises out of our feeling worthless.

In order for us to feel valuable and important, two things must be true. Larry Crabb defines these two things in his book, "THE MARRIAGE BUILDER."[1] Dr. Crabb says, *"That in order to feel valuable and important, a person must feel both secure and significant."*

He defines security as a *"convinced awareness of being unconditionally and totally loved without needing to change in order to win love, loved by a love that is freely given, that cannot be earned, and, therefore, cannot be lost."* If we are loved by that kind of unconditional love, then our soul will be satisfied. The only One in the universe Who can love us that way is Jesus Christ. But when we have not experienced His love, then that security is not there, and we don't sense the value, worth, and importance that He wants us to have.

In order to feel valuable, we must also feel a sense of significance. Larry Crabb defines significance as *"a realization that I am engaged in a responsibility or job that is truly important, whose results will not evaporate with time, but will last through eternity, that fundamentally involves having a meaningful impact on another person, a job for which I am completely adequate."*

Once again, Jesus Christ is the only One Who can provide us with this kind of significance. By trusting Him and relying on Him, we feel value through Him.

So whenever we believe the lie that we are unimportant not only to God, but also to other people, we feel worthless and fear results.

1 John 4:18 tells us, *"There is no fear in love, but perfect love casts out fear. Fear has torment, and he that fears is not made in perfect love."* You experience torment when you feel worthless and valueless. Maybe you've had an experience with somebody's pushing you out of his or her way. Somebody crowds in front of you in line, and you feel worthless and valueless. Maybe an authority in your life, a parent or your boss, chastises you and makes you feel worthless.

When the fear that you are a worthless person torments you, your flesh is compelled to react. Your soul can't just remain in that torment, and your flesh tries to do something to quench it.

The <u>second question</u> that we ask is: *"Will my needs be met? Will my goals be fulfilled?"* This has to do with our physical needs, our emotional needs, our intellectual needs, every type of need that we have in our lives. Jesus Christ wants to be the source of meeting every need. He says in His Word that He is faithful to meet us in every need that we have.

But when we are uncertain that our needs have been met, we find it very difficult to trust God. Deep down fear results. Once again, we are tormented by the fear that our needs will not be met.

When that happens, the flesh rises up in reaction to try to quench that torment. In desperation it suggests something that you should do to make certain that your own needs are met.

An even greater lie underlies these two lies and fears that you are of no value and that your needs will not be met. Satan tries to make you believe, deep down inside, that God does not love you. Do you remember 1 John 4:18 said that perfect love casts out all fear? Fear results when we don't receive the perfect love of God. The lie that God doesn't love us comes from people and circumstances. It may come through our parents, brothers and sisters, school teachers, university professors. It even comes from the pulpit in the church. **It comes to us that God's love is dependent upon our performance.** Then we experience that our performance is not sufficient, and we find ourselves lacking and inadequate to earn God's love. So we feel worthless and valueless and believe God doesn't love us. Then we listen to what our flesh tells us will make us feel better. And this is exactly how we get in bondage to habits.

When we're in bondage to a habit, our flesh then tells us that we are unworthy. And we feel guilty, condemned, and ashamed before God because of the habit.

It was through these lies that the devil entrapped Eve in the Garden of Eden (Genesis 3:4, 5). Satan told Eve that God was withholding from her the very thing that she needed: God did not want her to be wise, to know what He knew. He wanted her to be subservient to Him, to be a slave, a nothing in the Garden that He had created. The devil said God had told her not to eat of the fruit, not because He loved her and it would be bad for her, but because it was something that would be very good for her. In summary, God didn't really love her and wanted to withhold that which was good for her.

Eve began to believe those lies. She began to doubt that God really loved her or that He would meet her needs. Furthermore, Eve began to doubt that she was valuable and important. As a result, she rebelled against God; she partook of the fruit; and sin entered the world.

WHY DO WE BELIEVE THESE LIES?

Often it seems that our past experiences have confirmed that God is not faithful. Many people have said to me, *"Well, my experience has been that everything I try to do fails. I pray to God and ask Him, even beg Him, to help me, but it doesn't appear that He helps me."* These people believe that their past experiences have confirmed conclusively that God is not faithful.

The problem with this kind of thinking is that these people are using their natural minds to interpret experiences. They are not trusting in revelation from the Holy Spirit. Their natural minds have simply interpreted information from their five senses and have drawn an untruthful conclusion about Who God is, who they are, who other people are, or the reality of the circumstances.

For example, suppose a little four-year-old girl sees her dad out in the back yard building something with a hammer and nails. She grabs hold of one of the boards and tries to hold it for him so he can nail two boards together.

The father does not understand what the little daughter is doing and, consumed with the project, tells her to go away. He tells her he is very busy, to stop bothering him, and to go back inside the house.

The little girl probably would be devastated by her father's reacting to her in this way. Her five senses would feed her information. She would see the stern expression on her father's face and hear his harsh words. Her feelings would be hurt because of his rejection. He continues on in his project, not knowing that he just devastated his little daughter's emotions. Because of that experience, she then begins to believe things about herself that are not the truth. She has interpreted a circumstance based upon information gathered by her five senses, her natural mind, without revelation by the Holy Spirit.

First of all, she might begin to believe that she is a worthless and valueless person. Her father just proved it to her. She believes that her father is very busy and has critical projects to do, and she is unimportant to him. Projects are more important to him than she is. She decides not to open herself up to him again to be hurt in that same way.

These are all lies that have been based on a terrible misunderstanding. But the little girl may establish an image of herself by interpreting this experience in this particular way, rather than going to God and saying, *"Father, I need revelation from You. What's the truth about my earthly father? What's the truth about me? Who am I?"*

If she does not do this, as she gets older, she will begin to attribute the feeling she believes her father has about her to her heavenly Father too. She will also believe that other men will treat her the same way that her father has.

As the little girl grows up, she may experience more rejection from men. She may also experience rejection from other authorities: school teachers, boyfriends, and eventually a husband, should she marry. She may draw out of men the same rejection that she experienced with her father, because she believes deep inside that she is worthless.

Since she believes the lie that she is worthless and valueless and that God doesn't really love her, she has experiences as she grows up that confirm to her what she believes. She keeps interpreting experiences that happen in her life according to past experiences that were interpreted incorrectly by her natural mind.

Believing the lies that God doesn't love you, that you are not valuable, and because He doesn't love you, He is not going to be faithful to meet your needs, is the deception of sin in your flesh that leads you into unbelief and distrust toward God. Nobody can trust somebody whom he/she believes is not faithful. If you believe deep inside that you have conclusive evidence from past experiences that God has not met your needs and, therefore, He probably won't meet your needs now, it is impossible for you to trust Him. You can't trust someone who you believe doesn't have your best interest at heart. A man would be a fool to trust his life to someone who is far more powerful than he is, but does not have his best interest at heart.

So the deception of sin through the interpretation by the natural mind of the experience of the past creates the unbelief and hardness of heart that makes it impossible to trust God. Unconditional love has not been experienced. Instead, fear still torments so that the soul is not at rest or in peace. Therefore, the flesh is compelled to do something to attempt to bring peace.

Often people speak words to us that are not the truth, not in accordance with what God says. If we receive those things and believe them, they become established as images in our minds as well. In time, rather than believing the truth that God speaks to us, we believe false premises that have become established within us. These false beliefs often confirm our worst fears.

If you experience yourself as worthless and valueless, your flesh naturally reacts and says, *"Exalt yourself. Make yourself greater and more powerful and more important than that fear of being worthless."*

For example, the parents of a teenager may confirm their child's feelings of unimportance through anger and a critical attitude. The fear of worthlessness may then stimulate the young person to look for acceptance and importance through drugs, sex, or other destructive behavior. In his attempt to create value through these methods, he will actually further destroy his own sense of self-worth.

When we sin, our God-given conscience accuses us, and guilt begins to plague us. The guilt then creates a lack of peace in the soul, and the flesh again goes to work to come up with another solution to bring the soul into peace. The young person then ends up in a never-ending, destructive cycle of worthlessness, sin, guilt, condemnation, fear, worthlessness, etc.

The flesh then says, *"Do whatever you need to do to get your needs met."* The essence of that is rebellion: governing and controlling your own life, doing whatever you need to do to get your needs met.

---

[1]Lawrence J. Crabb, Jr., Phd., *The Marriage Builder,* (Grand Rapids,: Zondervan, 1982), p. 29.

CHAPTER 2

WHY HAVE I BEEN UNABLE TO OVERCOME MY BAD HABITS?

Deep down in our hearts, we believe we have the power to change habits, to modify our conduct and behavior, and to control our lives. We believe that by the power of our own wills, we can start and stop anything. So we use our own strength to try to overcome habits. It doesn't work, because the Bible guarantees us that the law of sin in our flesh is more powerful than our own will power to overcome sin. **The truth is that only the power of the blood of Jesus Christ can overcome sin and terminate wrong attitudes and habits from operating in our lives.**

In order to understand how these sinful attitudes and habits operate within us, let's look at how God created us. 1 Thessalonians 5:23 says:

> *"Now may the God of peace himself sanctify you entirely and may your **spirit** and **soul** and **body** be preserved complete without blame at the coming of the Lord Jesus Christ."*

The Bible tells us in the book of Genesis that we were created in God's image. God is a three part being, and thus we are also three part beings. While He is Father, Son, and Holy Spirit, we are spirit, soul, and body. Jesus said that God is a Spirit, and those who worship Him must worship Him in spirit and in truth. Likewise, man is a spiritual being. We are spirits; we have souls; and we live in bodies.

WHAT IS THE DIFFERENCE BETWEEN THE SPIRIT AND THE SOUL?

Many people believe that there isn't any difference between the spirit and the soul. However, Hebrews 4:12 states that the Word of God is sharper than any two-edged sword, piercing the **division of the spirit and soul.**

Your spirit enables you to know God. You can know **about** God in your soul, but you know Him **personally** in your spirit. You can receive revelation knowledge from God in your spirit, which is that part of you that communes with God and in which your conscience resides.

Your spirit contains the ability to know right from wrong. The spirit is what differentiates man from animals. Animals are only two-part beings: they have a soul and a body, but they don't have spirits. They are driven by instincts, that is,by dictates within their own souls. But man is a spiritual being; he knows right from wrong. Man is a moral being and possesses the ability to know God. Man's spirit will live eternally.

The soul (mind, will, and emotions) is that part of us in which we live most of our lives. It is where we think and make our choices. Our souls can receive information either from the five senses or by revelation knowledge from the spirit, or both. The body houses both the spirit and the soul.

II Corinthians 5:17 says:

> *"Therefore, if any man is in Christ, he is a new creature, the old things have passed away, behold new things have come."*

This describes what happens when we are born again; we become new creatures or new creations. The old things have passed away, and new ones have come. You may have noticed that there are certain areas of your life that did not "become new" at the new birth. Often you don't feel like a new creation; rather, you feel like the same old creation that you were before you were born again. So what has become new? Did you receive a new body? No, you have the same body as before. Did you receive a new soul? A new intellect? A new will? A new set of emotions or feelings? No, you also have the same soul that you had before you were born again. Now certain areas of your soul might be instantly renewed, but you didn't get an entirely new soul at the new birth.

So what is new? Only your spirit was made new or recreated when you were born again. The Bible says that the spirit passes from death and darkness into life and light at the new birth. Romans 6:6 says the "body of sin" was destroyed. Our spirits were purged of sin and recharged with the incorruptible seed, which is of the nature of the Lord Jesus Christ, Who is the living and abiding Word of God. (See 1 Peter 1:23)

Your human spirit desires to dominate and govern your soul. Now your flesh, which contains a remnant of sin, is used to governing your soul and does not want to relinquish that authority. Consequently, a battle ensues:

> *"But I say walk by the spirit and you will not carry out the desire of the flesh, for the flesh sets its desire against the spirit and the spirit against the flesh. For these are in opposition against one another so that you may not do the things that you please." (Galatians 5: 16, 17)*

So we see that our souls can be governed either by our flesh or by our recreated, born-again spirits. The recreated spirit cannot reproduce anything other than the nature of the Lord Jesus Christ. Every seed reproduces only after its own kind; for example, an orange tree always reproduces oranges, and an apple tree always reproduces apples. An orange tree does not produce apples - and never will. Likewise, the seed of the Lord Jesus Christ, the living and abiding Word of God Who dwells in our spirits, cannot reproduce anything but the nature of the Lord Jesus Christ.

The flesh sets its will against the spirit and desires to govern your soul to keep you from doing the very things that your spirit wants you to do. However, if you walk in the spirit - let your recreated, born-again spirit govern your soul - then it is not possible for you to carry out the desires of your flesh. Your flesh and spirit cannot rule simultaneously; only one can dominate at a time. If you allow your soul to be governed by your spirit, it is not possible for your flesh to govern in the same area.

In Romans 7:21-23 Paul describes how most of us battle against habits and against wrong attitudes in our lives. Paul also tells us why this method of battling against sin does not work. The wrong attitudes and habits that govern us do not emanate from our born-again spirits and ultimately bring us captive to their own dictates. They don't come from the nature of Jesus Christ in the spirit; rather, these habits and attitudes come from sin that resides in the flesh. This sin is deceitful and rises up to capture us:

> *"For sin taking opportunity through the commandment deceived me and through it killed me." (Romans 7:11)*

The sin, which resides in the flesh, rises up in response to that dissatisfaction, to the lack of peace in the soul, deceives the emotions first, then the intellect, and then the will. In this way, sin captures the soul and operates through it.

In Romans 7:21-23 Paul states:

> *"I find then the principal that evil is present in me, the one who wishes to do good. For I joyfully concur with the law*

27

of God in the inner man, but I see a different law in the members of my body, waging war against the law of my mind, and making me a prisoner of the law of sin which is in my members."

Where is that evil? It dwells in the flesh. But Paul says evil **is** present in him, the one who wishes to do good. In reality, Paul is a spirit - recreated and born again by the blood of the Lord Jesus Christ - who wishes to do good. However, the evil, which resides in Paul's flesh, does not agree with the law of God; and in verse 23 Paul sees a different law at war within himself.

Paul describes three different laws in verses 22 and 23: (1) the law of God, with which he joyfully agrees and concurs, (2) the law of sin and death, which dwells within his flesh and seeks to take him captive, and (3) the law of the mind.

HOW DOES GOD EXPECT US TO DRAW CONCLUSIONS?

The law of the mind is any standard of behavior or of conduct or of thinking that you take, be it right or wrong, and then attempt to perform it. In other words, we can take standards from our parents, our peers, our friends, our church members, our pastors, or even from the Word of God Itself, and try to make them laws in our minds. Paul is saying that, since the law of sin in our members is more powerful than any law that we put in our minds and attempt to do, action based on these self-imposed laws is guaranteed to fail.

1 Corinthians 2:14 states:

> *"But a natural man does not accept the things of the Spirit of God; for they are foolishness to him and he cannot understand them, because they are spiritually appraised."*

There are two sources of information: (1) revelation knowledge from God, and (2) information from your five senses. Your natural mind receives information from your five senses, evaluates it, and draws conclusions. However, the natural mind does not understand spiritual information, because it is foolishness to the natural mind.

God desires that we know the truth in circumstances, about other people, and about Himself - not by interpreting those circumstances with our own natural minds, but by receiving revelation knowledge from Him.

If our natural minds understand the Word of God, we will then use it as a law in our minds and try to perform it by the power of our own strengths and wills. However, this method always fails. Instead, God intends for us to receive revelation knowledge from His word, **to build our faith in Him.** This very faith will set us free. God is our Deliverer: He is the only

One Who has power to set us free and deliver us from any bondage to wrong habits and attitudes.

Through the power of the blood of Jesus Christ, we can be set free from the power of a habit or wrong attitude. However, we commonly take the Word of God, make it a standard or a law in our minds, and attempt to accomplish it through our own strengths. The end result is failure. Then we blame God and believe that He is not helping us. Ultimately, we come into condemnation and shame. That law has then brought death into our minds and emotions, rather than the life and freedom we thought it would bring.

The natural mind is governed by the flesh. The natural mind does not accept the things of the Spirit of God, because they are foolishness to it. For example, the Bible says that our bodies are the temple of the Holy Spirit. We realize that drinking alcohol defiles our bodies and gives our emotions, minds, and wills over to some control other than the Lord Jesus Christ, so we decide that we should not drink alcoholic beverages. We make that a law in our minds, and then we try to perform that law by repeating, "I'm not going to drink. I'm not going to drink!"

We attempt to use the power of our wills, to try to overcome our desire to drink. But as Paul said in Romans 7:23, the law in your mind will not overcome the law of sin and death, and you will fail. You will be disappointed, discouraged, and defeated. Then the devil will tempt you to blame God for your failure.

If we had power to perform the Word of God in our own strengths and wills, God would not have expended the precious blood of His son, the Lord Jesus Christ. God would simply have sent someone who could explain to us how to overcome sin in our lives.

However, the fact is that we do not have that power. Therefore, God sent Jesus Christ to die on the cross for us, to shed His blood that He might make us new creatures in the spirit. Through His spilled blood, we have power to live and to walk in the spirit. No longer must we attempt to overcome sin in our lives through the strength of our own willpower.

WHAT HAPPENS WHEN WE TRY TO PERFORM LAWS IN OUR OWN MINDS?

Let's say, for example, that you read a scripture that convicts you of a particular sin in your life. Naturally, realizing that your behavior is sin and is not pleasing to God, you decide that you are going to change. You set up a standard in your mind saying, "I am going to stop this sin from operating in my life." Later, you catch yourself doing the very thing that you were not going to do. And you think, "Oh, I'm sinning. I need to stop." So you try to stop your habit by sheer willpower, and you notice that even as you focus on not doing something, in reality, you are focusing on the very thing that causes you to sin.

At this point you may begin to cry out to God and beg Him, "Lord, help me to stop doing this. Make me strong, Lord!" And you believe that by crying out to God, you are trusting in Him. But you are not trusting

31

Him at all -- **you are still trusting in your own will to overcome your bad habit.** You are neither dwelling in nor walking in the spirit. You are not abiding in God nor receiving His love. You are not believing the truth of who He has said you are already recreated to be in the spirit. Instead, you are begging Him to strengthen your will so that you will not continue to sin. All the while, as you are focusing on not sinning, the sin actually seems to take an increasingly powerful hold on your mind and behavior. Anyone who has ever been on a diet understands this principle .

The more you meditate upon not allowing yourself to fall into sin, the more powerful the habit becomes in your mind. Your flesh tells you that satisfying the compulsion will bring you peace and comfort. Eventually, you become convinced that God is not going to help you, and you go ahead to do the very thing that you were determined not to do. You believe that He is not bringing you peace nor comfort, and your flesh has convinced you that nothing will set you free from the awful torment of your habit.

Afterward, you feel terribly condemned and ashamed. You are disappointed in yourself, and you believe that God, too, must be disappointed in you. This is not the truth! God loves us:

> *"But God demonstrates His own love toward us, in that while we were yet sinners, Christ died for us" (Romans 5:8)*

God's love is unconditional and unchangeable. He loves us regardless of our habits or wrong attitudes. But because you feel so disappointed and ashamed before God, you believe that He feels the same toward you. You believe that other people are condemning you, and you feel ashamed before them as well.

Then you believe that because you failed to overcome that habit, the sin that was producing the habit is more powerful than the power of Jesus Christ within you. So you do one of two things: (1) give up and decide that it is not possible to overcome your habit or (2) start the cycle all over again by determining in your heart that you are just going to have to try harder to overcome that particular problem.

And what you really will be doing is trying to use your flesh to fight your flesh. You will be using your natural mind to understand the Word of God -- to set up a standard in your own mind -- and then you will attempt to overcome your problem by the power and strength of your own will. When you fail, you blame God and become angry with Him, because you believe that He is not helping you. This is exactly the deception that Paul describes in Romans 7:11:

> *"For sin, taking opportunity through the commandment, deceived me, and through it killed me."*

For example, let's say that someone falsely accuses you of something. That person is trying to destroy your reputation with others, and hatred begins to rise up in your heart toward the person who is accusing you. You want him to be punished for hurting you.

But the Word of God says that we are to love our enemies -- not hate them. You receive the Word in your natural mind, and you say, "Oh, hatred and anger are in me. The Bible says that I should forgive this person." You make the Word a law in your mind and say, "Okay, I'm going to forgive and walk in love toward this person."

Soon your natural mind begins to devise a plan to do this. Perhaps you do a study in 1 Corinthians 13. Perhaps you decide to take the person out to lunch as an act of friendship toward him. Yet, deep down in your heart, you are still angry with this person for maligning you. During your luncheon engagement your hurt feelings begin to show, and you want him to apologize for hurting you. But the person, picking up on your intentions, hardens his heart even more and refuses to apologize. Your plan has backfired, and you find yourself becoming even angrier. You leave the luncheon feeling self-righteous and self-justified, and you say to the Lord, "I've done the right thing. I tried to love that person, but he is still treating me unfairly. Lord, I am being persecuted for Your name's sake."

Through this process you enter into works of righteousness. You justify yourself through your own works -- not the works of Jesus Christ coming through you! You alone are trying to rid yourself of that hatred and anger. Your works will not bring life to your soul. Rather than cleansing your emotions or your mind, your works are simply bringing you deeper and deeper in bondage.

We expect that anger and hatred will magically disappear, because we are trying to act in love. But when those feelings don't disappear, we get angry at the Lord, because He doesn't seem to help us overcome our feelings. We feel disappointed and condemned and ashamed before God once again, because we know we shouldn't hate another person. Yet we are feeling hatred and apparently cannot rid ourselves of it.

Soon we think, "I'm a horrible person. The Bible says that if I won't forgive others, God won't forgive me." And we begin to think, "God isn't going to forgive me, because I'm so full of hatred. I can't come before the Lord, because I can't get rid of this hatred that I'm feeling." We begin to fall into the very cycle that Paul describes in Romans 7:21-23: we set up a law in our minds. It's true that we should love others, but when we try to do it through sheer willpower, we fail. Then we get angry at God and become disappointed in ourselves. We focus on the problem and become completely conscious of the sin that's within us rather than conscious of who Jesus Christ is within us. We'll never be able to overcome a wrong attitude or habit in our lives through willpower.

WHAT IS THE BASIS OF MY PROBLEM?

Fear is the underlying torment that motivates bad habits or wrong attitudes in your live. The reason you feel anger or hatred toward the person maligning your reputation is because you don't feel valuable or important. Your value is not established in the truth of who you are in Jesus Christ. You feel even more worthless when this other person gossips about you. You want to defend yourself to others who may have heard the nasty rumors, and you want to make the person stop spreading them.

Pride rises up out of your flesh to exalt yourself and to counteract the things that the person is saying about you. His false accusations stimulate fear and lack of peace, because you are not at peace with your identity in Jesus Christ. The pride is working to try to defend yourself, and the hatred and anger are coming out of that pride - your flesh needs to defend you, because your soul is not at rest.

As long as the fear is still there, the hatred and anger will not leave. Why? Because they are protecting you from experiencing the torment and the pain of the fear of being worthless that's being stimulated by what the other person is saying. Fear isn't going to go away just by trying to love the other person. The only way that it will go away is by repenting of the pride that's operating within you, of the fear in your heart that you are worthless, and of the unbelief that God is not faithful and doesn't value you. **True repentance is the only thing that releases the unconditional love of the Lord Jesus Christ:**

> *"There is no fear in love; but perfect love casts out fear, because fear involves*

punishment, and the one who fears is not perfected in love." (1 John 4:18)

When the torment is gone, your flesh no longer needs to operate in pride, hatred, or anger toward the other person. When the fear is gone, the torment is gone and you are at rest with Jesus Christ.

In every case, a bad habit develops as a means of covering up the torment and the pain of feeling worthless and feeling that your needs are not going to be met. When you allow Jesus Christ to be your Source and to meet your needs, His love will cast out that fear. The torment will depart, and the need for the habit or the wrong attitude will disappear. You are able to overcome your habits and wrong attitudes by walking in the spirit and by receiving the unconditional love of the Lord.

Recently the Lord revealed this to me in an area of my own life. He showed me that I had been using food to comfort my soul. At certain times, particularly weekends, I would feel a certain listlessness or boredom in my soul. I didn't really experience it consciously; yet it was there. And I noticed that when I would have that feeling, I would begin to eat. The Lord convicted me that I was not eating for nutritional purposes; rather I was eating to comfort my soul. I was trusting in food rather than in Jesus to bring me peace. Consequently, I was gaining weight.

I tried to stop eating that food simply by making a law in my mind and saying, "I'm not going to snack between meals." However, invariably, I would become dissatisfied in my soul, and my flesh would tell me, "Just eat a bowl of ice cream, and you'll feel much better." And I would eat a bowl of ice cream and feel better - temporarily. Later my flesh would demand more food, and I continually ate more and more to satisfy my flesh.

The flesh is never satisfied with just the one thing that you believe is going to satisfy you. Your flesh defrauds you - it doesn't deliver what it says. It claims that it will deliver peace and satisfaction to your soul, but it never does. It brings only temporary peace and eventually demands more.

When the Holy Spirit revealed that I had developed a bad habit of snacking and overeating, I began to concentrate on **not** eating. With each passing moment, I became more aware of my hunger. The more I tried not to eat, the more I thought about eating. I became so conscious of the problem and its gnawing "power" over me, that finally I couldn't stand it any longer, and I ate.

The Holy Spirit revealed that instead of making a law in my mind to stop eating, I needed simply to abide in the spirit. Instead of trusting in food, I needed to begin trusting in Jesus to be my Source, my Lord, and my Deliverer. God showed me that my trust in food was idolatrous - I was making food my god and not allowing Jesus to be Lord over my eating. I needed to yield to Jesus rather than my flesh to bring me comfort and peace and to satisfy the anguish and torment in my soul that my needs would not be met.

When the Lord convicted me that I had been using a law in my own mind to try to control my eating, I was able to repent of fear, rebellion toward the Lord, and lack of trust in Him to bring me comfort and peace. As quickly as I repented and began to trust Jesus, I became free of habitual snacking and overeating. Glory to God!

CHAPTER 3

WHAT ARE THE KEYS TO BREAK THE BONDAGE?

1) Do not identify yourself in the flesh.

The primary deceptive tool Satan uses is to cause us to self-identify with sin. For example, we may recognize that our flesh has control in some area of our lives and choose to agree with the devil that our true identity is defined by our sinful behavior. In so doing we are identifying ourselves according to our flesh rather than according to our true nature in the spirit. We say, "I am just a critical person," or "I am frequently depressed," or "I have always been prone to lust," or "that is just my temperament."

Apostle Paul tells us in II Corinthians 5:14-17:

> *"For the love of Christ controls us, having concluded this, that one died for all, therefore all died; and He died for all that they who live should no longer live for themselves, but for Him who died and rose again on their behalf. Therefore, from now on we recognize not man according to the flesh; even though we have known Christ according to the flesh, yet now we know Him thus no longer. Therefore, if any man is in Christ, he is a new creature; the old*

41

*things passed away; behold, new things
have come."*

You must allow the love of Jesus Christ to control
you and refuse to identify with your flesh. Let Jesus'
love control you. Paul then says that you are not to
recognize any man according to the flesh. This
certainly starts with you! You are not to recognize
yourself according to the flesh, no matter the external
manifestation; rather, you must begin to identify
yourself as a spirit man, as the true spirit man that you
are in Jesus Christ.

It is this identifying of ourselves in the spirit and
not according to the flesh, even when the flesh is
currently manifesting itself in our behavior, that
Apostle Paul speaks about in Romans 7:14-20. In this
passage, Paul describes the battle in his soul between
what his recreated spirit wishes to do and what his
flesh compels him to do. *"But if I am doing the very
thing I do not wish, am I no longer the one doing it,
but sin which dwells in me."* (Rom. 7:20) Here Paul has
disassociated his personal identity (I, the spirit man,
who wishes), from sin in his flesh (I, the soul man
captured by the flesh, who does.)

In this passage, Paul uses the word "I" many times,
but is actually describing different parts of his being.
Below I have written the passage with each "I"
amplified to describe which part of his being I believe
Paul is speaking about.

"For that which I, (the soul), am doing, I (the spirit), do not understand; for I, (the soul), am not practicing what I, (the spirit), would like to do, but I, (the soul), am doing the very thing I (the spirit), hate. But if I, (the soul), do the very thing I, (the spirit), do not wish to do, I, (the spirit), agree with the Law, confessing that is good. so now no longer am I, (the spirit), the one doing it, but sin which indwells me, (in my flesh). for I know that nothing good dwells in me, that is in my flesh; for the wishing is present in me, (the spirit and soul together), but the doing, (in the soul), is not. For the good that I, (the spirit and soul together), wish I, (the soul), do not do; but I,(the soul), practice the very evil that I, (the spirit and soul together) do not wish, I, (the spirit), am no longer the one doing it, but sin which dwells in me, (in my flesh)." (Rom. 7:15-20)

In disassociating his personal identity from sin in his flesh, Apostle Paul is viewing sin, in a sense, almost as something external to himself, like the unauthorized invasion of a foreign object. If a particle of dust flies into my eye, I would never identify myself with it, I would not say that it is a part of me. I would not simply accept blurred vision and watering eyes as the way vision is for me. No! Of course not. I would regard the particle of dust as a foreign object which has invaded my physical body without authorization, and would immediately take measures to remove it.

I am not saying that we are absolved from responsibility when sin manifests through us. Unlike a particle of dust entering the eye, sin does pass through our will, and we do make a conscious choice to let it operate, albeit most of the time it is through deception. Nonetheless, we are responsible for the choices we make. *"The soul (not spirit) who sins will die."* (Ezek. 18:4)

However, there are two very important reasons why we should not identify ourselves with sin in our flesh.

1. The Bible tells us that we should have God's attitude toward sin. We then quickly discover that God's attitude toward sin is hatred. It is an abomination to Him. If I must have God's attitude toward sin, then I must hate it, too. Now if I identify myself with sin, operating through my flesh, and I believe that sin is I, then whom must I hate? Myself, of course.

When you hate yourself, you feel very ashamed and disappointed in yourself, and you usually believe that God feels about you the same that you feel about yourself. Then you won't run to Him in repentance or receive His forgiveness and let Him set you free. Instead, you try to stop the sin yourself, so that you can then come to God without shame and feel right before Him. You then fail all the more, because you don't have the power to stop it, and you have through fear and shame cut yourself off from the only One Who has power to deliver you. The more you fail, the more you identify yourself with the sin and become convinced that it really is you and will never change.

2. When sin manifests through your soul, it is the fruit of your flesh. In every piece of fruit are many seeds. When you identify sin in your flesh as being you, you plant that fruit and all the seed within it in the soil of your soul. If there are 10 seeds in the fruit, and each seed produces a tree bearing 100 new pieces of fruit, you can very quickly see a 1000-fold multiplication of that kind of fruit in your life.

> *"Do not be deceived. God is not mocked; for whatever a man sows, this he will also reap. For the one who sows to his own flesh shall from the flesh reap corruption, but the one who sows to the Spirit shall from the Spirit reap eternal life."* (Gal. 6:7-8)

> *"For we walk by faith and not by sight"* (II Corinthians 5:7)

The Amplified Bible gives us a definition of faith in Hebrews 1:1:

> *"(Faith is) perceiving as real fact what is not revealed to senses."*

God wants you to walk by faith and to perceive as real fact what is already true in the spirit, but is not yet revealed to or experienced by the senses. You are to agree with who God says you are, not who you experience yourself to be with your five senses.

So we see that when we disassociate our personal identity from sin in our flesh, we are free to have God's attitude toward sin and toward ourselves. I can hate sin without hating myself and thus be free to run to my Heavenly Father and let Him love me and set me free. If, after repenting and receiving forgiveness, I then identify myself with the true nature of my recreated spirit, Christ in me, the hope of glory (Col. 1:27), I am then nullifying the fruit of my flesh and sowing the fruit of my recreated spirit into my soul.

2) Receive the fear of the Lord and the hatred of sin.

> *"The fear of the Lord is the beginning of wisdom. And the knowledge of the Holy One is understanding."* (Proverbs 9:10)

The fear of the Lord being talked about here is not being afraid of God. It is talking about a reverence for God and a respect for His opinion. Fearing the Lord has to do with coming into agreement with God's attitudes and opinions.

> *"The fear of the Lord is to hate evil: Pride and arrogance and the evil way, and the perverted mouth I hate."* (Proverbs 8:13)

Here the fear of the Lord is defined as the hatred of evil. In order to receive your freedom, you must agree with God not only in His love for you but also in His hatred of sin. Many times we don't hate our sin, but deep inside we secretly enjoy it. You will never get free of the bondage to your flesh until you hate it with the hatred of God. If you don't really hate your sin, pray and ask the Lord to give you His attitude toward your sin. You must hate that sin so much that you are willing to bring your flesh to the cross and let it die. If you don't, you'll never release the resurrection life of the Lord Jesus from your spirit into your soul, you'll remain in bondage to your flesh.

Sin is a grievous and destructive force. Often we don't hate it, because we don't realize how destructive it is, and what it does to the heart of God. I once heard an analogy which is somewhat descriptive of Jesus' death on the cross for our sin. It goes like this. There was a man who operated a drawbridge in a port city in which large ocean liners would sail up the river and under his drawbridge. Often times in the summer months, the man's 10-year-old son would help him open and close the drawbridge.

One day a large passenger liner filled with people returning from a cruise came steaming toward the bridge. The operator pushed the button to raise the bridge, but nothing happened. Quickly, he looked over the side and spotted the problem. A wrench had fallen down amidst the huge gears and was preventing them from turning. The man's son saw the problem, too, and could see that if someone didn't do something, the bridge would not rise and the ship would hit it and kill many of the people on board. The son quickly climbed over the side and said to his dad, "I'll get the wrench, so you can raise the bridge." The man anxiously watched his son disappear over the side. The ship was still coming full speed ahead expecting the bridge to open at any moment. The man watched his son struggle to remove the wrench from the gears. At last he got it free, but it was too late. The ship was almost to the bridge. If the man waited another five seconds, it would be too late, and the ship would hit the bridge killing many people. On the other hand, if he raised the bridge now, he would trap his little son in the huge gears and crush him. He heard his son cry out, "Daddy, open the bridge before it's too late." He hesitated one more second, and then he hit the button to raise the bridge.

As the ship passed by, all the passengers were standing on deck, waving cheerfully to the bridge operator, drinking their Pina Coladas, and merrily dancing. The operator, however stood in the control house with tears in his eyes, watching the ship pass by. He did not wave or drink or dance.

Your sin has cost the Lord Jesus His life. Let the Father show you the seriousness of your own sin, so that you can hate it as He does. You can only really receive the love of the Father to the same extent that you have received the hatred of evil. With the fear of the Lord will come a conviction of sin and godly sorrow.

3) Repent of sin, and die to your flesh.

"For the sorrow that is according to the will of God produces a repentance without regret, leading to salvation; but the sorrow of the world produces death."
(II Cor. 7:10)

Godly sorrow will lead you to repentance, which will release the blood of Christ to cleanse, heal and deliver. You must repent of the following:

(A) The external manifestation of sin (i.e., the habit). Renounce it and ask the Lord to forgive you for letting it operate and for trusting in it to bring you peace and comfort.

(B) Pride. Renounce pride and your seeking to establish your own identity in yourself and your own works. Renounce trying to deliver yourself by the power of your own will. That's pride - trust in yourself. Colossians 2:10 tells us that "In Him you have been made complete." You must repent of believing the lie that you are not of value. You are as valuable as the life of Jesus Christ, because that is what your Father paid for you.

(C) Rebellion. Renounce rebellion and seeking to deliver yourself by the power of your own will. Renounce doing whatever you need to do to comfort your own soul and meet your own needs. Repent and ask the Lord to forgive you. Isaiah 50:10-11 says to stop trying to kindle your own fire. Jesus Christ is well able to meet every need you have, if you'll trust Him.

(D) Unbelief and distrust toward God. Renounce unbelief. Renounce fear. Ask God to forgive you for not trusting Him to meet your needs and establish your value. Ask Him to forgive you for not letting Him comfort you and bring your soul into peace.

> *"And now, little children, abide in Him, so that when He appears, we may have confidence and not shrink away from Him in shame at His coming." (1 John 2:28)*

He has come to you many times to be your peace and comfort, but you have shrunk away from Him in shame. Repent now for not trusting Him and for shrinking away in shame, fear, and unbelief.

As you repent and ask the Lord's forgiveness, it is important that you receive His forgiveness. Let the blood of Jesus cleanse you now from guilt, shame, defilement and all uncleanness.

(E) Resisting the Father's love. Renounce your resistance of God's love. Repent of any anger you have held toward the Lord for seemingly not helping you. God has always been there for you. If you'll open yourself up to Him now, He'll show you why you thought He wasn't helping you. Ask the Lord to forgive you for resisting Him and not receiving His love for you.

Many times there are specific experiences that we have had in the past, particularly in childhood, in which we have been deeply hurt and interpreted at that time as God's not being faithful to us. These experiences confirm to us the lies of the devil, that we're not loved, not of value, and that our needs won't be met. Fear then enters in from our natural minds' interpretation of such experiences and torments the soul. This, then, gives rise to the working of the flesh.

The Holy Spirit may now want to give revelation of one or more of these past experiences through which fear and its torment have entered. Ask Him now if He would desire to do so. If He brings to your remembrance an experience that was painful, first let the emotion be expressed through you, if it is coming. Don't try to hold it in. Next, repent of the way you interpreted that experience, imputing unfaithfulness to God, and out of your pain establishing yourself in pride and rebellion.

The truth is that the Lord was there all the time, wanting to comfort you and speak the truth to you. But you couldn't receive His love at that time and hardened yourself against Him. Maybe you didn't even know to go to Him at all. Ask the Lord to speak to you now what He wanted to tell you then. Ask Him to give you the correct interpretation of the circumstance and to show you His absolute faithfulness to you in it. Let Him now bring your soul into peace.

Many times I have seen Christians get free of external bondages which have plagued them, when they have gotten revelation of deep seated unbelief toward God and inner torment, stemming from a past, devastating experience. One woman I know has had a serious problem with overeating and has become quite overweight. This problem, however, didn't begin until shortly after her brother, to whom she was quite close, died of cancer. You can easily see that this woman's soul is still being tormented and that her overeating is simply the flesh's reaction to the torment. She probably will not become free of the overeating until she gets revelation of the hurt, anger toward God, and perhaps guilt that are still unconsciously tormenting her soul.

Many of us have had devastating experiences of rejection and hurt from our parents and others in childhood and have never let the Lord uncover to us the fear and resulting torment that are still working unconsciously in the soul. Take this opportunity now to let the Father show to you anything that He wants to deal with. Don't use your natural mind to try to think something up, but if the Holy Spirit brings something to your remembrance, then deal with it.

(4) Receive God's love for you, and put your trust In Jesus Christ as your Deliverer. Let Him love you. Ask the Lord to speak to you now how He feels about you. Listen and receive from Him. Remember that perfect love casts out all fear. (1 John 4:18). Let Him bring your soul into peace. Rather than using the Word of God as a law in your mind, let the Word build faith in you toward Jesus as your Deliverer. Jesus Christ in your spirit is more powerful than the law of sin in your flesh.

Allow Jesus to become your Source of peace and joy. Receive His love and let Him be El Shaddai to you, which means "the God Who is more than enough." Jesus Christ is more than enough to meet every need. He can bring the comfort, peace, and joy that you have been seeking. And as you die to that habit, Jesus will become your Peace.

Remember Hebrews 4:10 proclaims:

> *"For the one who has entered His (God's) rest has himself also rested from his own works as God did from His."*

When you enter into God's rest, you will rest from your own works. You will be allowing Jesus Christ to be your Peace. Allow Him to tell you how valuable you really are to Him. Let Jesus show you how He desires to meet your needs.

And as you come into the revelation knowledge of the truth of Who Jesus is to you - Lord, God, Savior, Source of comfort, Source of having every need met, Source of value, significance and security - you will be receiving His perfect love, which will cast out any fear. Your soul will be at peace, and your flesh will have nothing negative to which it can react. You won't need that habit to bring you peace.

Jesus wasn't governed by his own flesh:

> *"Do you not believe that I am in the Father and the Father is in Me? The words that I say to you I do not speak on My own initiative, but the Father abiding in Me does His works." (John 14:10)*

Jesus' soul was at peace; therefore, his flesh did not constantly need to govern His soul and do something to try to bring peace. Instead, Jesus was abiding in His Father and allowing His Father to abide in Him. This brought His soul into peace and, as a result, He didn't do His own works. He did nothing on His own initiative, but, instead, He allowed Himself to rest in the peace of His Father, and His Father, abiding in Him, did the works through Him.

Jesus Christ wants you to trust Him to bring you that kind of peace. He will satisfy and bring you lasting peace - if you trust Him to deliver you and if you believe the truth of who you already are in the spirit. You simply need to release the "zoe" or "eternal life" of Jesus Christ, which resides in your spirit, to come forth into your soul and renew it:

> *"For indeed while we are in this tent (our physical bodies), we groan being burdened, because we do not want to be unclothed, but to be clothed, in order that what is mortal may be swallowed up by life" (II Cor. 5:4).*

We want that which is mortal to be swallowed by the life of God that dwells in our spirits. And that occurs as we trust in our Heavenly Father, rather than running away from Him. It happens as we believe the truth of who God says we already are rather than identifying with who we have been in the past and setting up a law in our minds to overcome it.

No, you already are set free:

> *"That the law of the spirit of life in Christ
> Jesus has set you free from the law of sin
> and death." (Romans 8:2)*

You simply need to allow that spirit life to come forth in you to flood your soul and renew your mind, so that you become in your outward manifestation and behavior what is already true in the spirit.

The manifestation of a compulsive habit indicates that your soul is not at rest and that you are not trusting Jesus Christ. That is not the time to run shamefully away from Him; rather, that's the time to run to Him! God is not ashamed of you even when you stumble spiritually. Run to Him and let the blood of Jesus Christ cleanse you. Then you press on to identify yourself according to the truth of who Jesus already says you are, and you will have victory over that habit! Jesus Christ in you is more powerful than any habit, than any wrong attitude, than any manifestation of sin through your flesh, and that habit will bow its knee to the power of the Lord Jesus Christ in your spirit when you trust in Him.

> *"If therefore the Son shall make you free,
> you shall be free indeed." (John 8:36)*

You won't want to miss the:
Family Foundations International Ancient Paths Seminar

What Is It?

An intensive time of teaching from God's word, followed by sharing, prayer, and ministry in small groups. As teaching topics are brought up, the small groups give opportunity for ministry in that specific area of the individual's life, marriage, or family. The seminar is conducted in a Thursday evening, Friday evening, and all day Saturday format.

Topics include

Communication
>	Recognizing different levels of communication.
>	Resolving Conflicts.

Purpose and Plan
>	Overview of God's plan and purposes for the individual and family.

Identity and Destiny
>	7 Critical Times of Blessing.

Life Patterns
>	8 Adult Life Patterns.
>	Impact of lack of blessing of the cursing of identity.

Cursing and Blessing
>	Releasing God's Blessing.
>	Practical steps to freedom from cursing.
>	Personal Ministry.

Vision Of Family Foundations

It is our vision and purpose to help re-impart back into the culture of the body of Christ, those safeguards which facilitate the natural impartation to people of identity and destiny from God, without such, the devil has been allowed to impart his message of worthlessness and purposelessness to millions of people throughout the earth.

Who should come?

Anyone desirous of lasting change in your life. Many times we see unpleasant, or unhealthy patterns in our lives, but don't know why they are there and/or can't seem to change. This ministry is designed to identify the root causes and bring lasting change to these areas.

For a schedule of future seminars or for information on how your church can schedule an Ancient Paths Seminar, please mail the attached form, call, and fax or contact us on the World Wide Web.

(303) 797 – 1139
(303) 797 – 1579 fax
www.familyfi.org
info@familyfi.org

Please send me information about the Ancient Paths Seminars.

Name _____
Address _____
City, State, Zip _____
Telephone _____

Mail to:
Family Foundations International
P.O. Box 320
Littleton, Colorado 80160

NOTES